Meditations for the
Twelve Great Feasts

Meditations for the Twelve Great Feasts

BECOMING FULLY HUMAN IN CHRIST

Vassilios Papavassiliou

ANCIENT FAITH PUBLISHING
CHESTERTON, INDIANA

Scripture quotations are taken from the New King James
Version, © 1979, 1980, 1982 by Thomas Nelson, Inc. Used
by permission.

Published by:
    Ancient Faith Publishing
    P.O. Box 748
    Chesterton, IN 46304
Printed in the United States of America

ISBN: 978-1-936270-26-2

Cover calligraphy by Jan Powell
Interior design by Katherine Hyde

Contents

A Guide to the Twelve Great Feasts

(Note: Julian "Old" Calendar dates are given following the Gregorian "New" Calendar dates throughout this book.)

The Nativity of the Mother of God
September 8/21
Fish is permitted if the feast falls on the Wednesday or Friday fast

The Elevation of the Cross
September 14/27
Fast day

The Entry of the Mother of God
November 21/December 4
Always falls in the Nativity Fast (Nov. 15–Dec. 24/Nov. 28–Jan. 6). Fish is permitted

The Nativity of our Lord
December 25/January 7
The period between the Nativity and the eve of Theophany is free of fasting

The Theophany
January 6/19
Fish is permitted if the feast falls on the Wednesday or Friday fast

The Meeting of the Lord
February 2/15
Fish is permitted if the feast falls on the Wednesday or Friday fast

The Annunciation of the Mother of God
March 25/April 7
Always falls during Great Lent. Fish is permitted on the Feast of the Annunciation

Palm Sunday
The Sunday before Pascha
The end of Lent and beginning of Holy Week. Fish is permitted on Palm Sunday

The Ascension of the Lord
Forty days after Pascha

Pentecost
Fifty days after Pascha
The week after Pentecost is free of fasting

The Transfiguration of the Lord
August 6/19

Always falls in the Dormition Fast (Aug. 1–14/14–27). Fish is permitted on the Feast of the Transfiguration

The Dormition of the Mother of God
August 15/28

Fish is permitted if the feast falls on the Wednesday or Friday fast

Introduction

IN EVERY AGE, IN EVERY CULTURE, regardless of religion, class, and status, human beings celebrate. Even in times of war and austerity, sorrow and pain, people will always thirst for celebration, for ritual, for remembrance. Man celebrates not because he has to in order to survive (there is nothing utilitarian or biologically necessary about celebration), but because it is human, and it expresses a deep longing in man to rejoice, to feel, to love and be loved, to belong, to be glad and whole.

This "unnecessary need" for celebration is not

something which the Church frowns upon as sinful or idle; on the contrary, the Church is full of celebration. The entire Church calendar is a year-long festivity, taking us from one feast to another, from one saint to the next; as soon as one season has ended, a new one begins.

At the heart of this annual cycle of celebrations is Pascha, the "Feast of Feasts." After this, great importance is attached the Twelve Great Feasts, which commemorate significant events in the life of our Lord Jesus Christ and of His Mother. A central theme which runs throughout all of these Great Feasts is God taking upon Himself the likeness of man, that man might acquire the likeness of God.

It is this fullness of humanity in God, through which we humans can become fully alive and one with God, that we celebrate in these Twelve Great Feasts. In them, we are called to recognize and worship the only One who is both fully God and fully man, the One who truly loves us as Himself and gave Himself up for us. In this recognition and adoration, in our response to all He has done for us, in our celebration, we discover what it means to be made in the image and likeness of God, what it means to love and be loved, and what it means to be fully human and fully alive.

Completely Human

THE NATIVITY OF THE MOTHER OF GOD

This is the day of the Lord; wherefore, rejoice all nations; for behold the chamber of Light, the scroll of the Word of life has come forth from the womb; the gate facing the east has been born. Wherefore, she awaits the entrance of the High Priest. And she alone admitted Christ into the world for the salvation of our souls. (Vespers, second troparion of the stichera)

WE WORSHIP A GOD WHO HAS A mother. This statement may seem paradoxical and nonsensical, but at its heart lies the very mystery of the Incarnation. The Nativity of the

Mother of God may seem at first glance to be a feast concerned solely with the Virgin Mary, but in Orthodox Christianity, every feast of the Theotokos is really a feast about the One to whom she gave birth: Jesus Christ. "God became what we are that we might become what He is."[1] So wrote St. Athanasius the Great, and it is the first part of this affirmation—"God became what we are"—that we are invited to contemplate whenever we celebrate the Birth of the Virgin Mary. She is singled out for veneration above every other saint, not on account of her holiness alone, but because it is through her that Christ entered the world.

But the mystery of the Incarnation does not end here. There is a danger in thinking of the Virgin Mary merely as a tool, a vessel, a means by which "the Word became flesh and dwelt among us" (John 1:14). Yet this "becoming flesh" meant

---

1   *On the Incarnation* 54.3 (Migne, Patrologia Graeca 25, 192 B: *De Incarnatione Verbi*, 54).

becoming not only a human body, but a complete human being: a human soul, a human mind, a human will, and everything else that is part and parcel of being truly human.

This includes going through infancy, being fed and nurtured, taught how to speak and how to walk. And although Christ as God, who bears all creation in the palm of His hand, had no need to be taught by anyone, He chose to condescend to the fullness of humanity and to subject Himself to everything we go through, with the exception of sin. The Virgin Mother was chosen to be not only the "Birth-giver of God" (Greek: *Theotokos*), but the "Mother of God" (Greek: *Meter tou Theou*). She gave Him the breast, reared Him, taught Him, and loved Him just as any mother does her child.

Whenever we wish to dehumanize someone, we tend to think of that person in isolation, forgetting that this person also has a mother, that he too was once an innocent baby. And when we wish to make people recognize that person's humanity—the inherent goodness that exists even in the most evil of people—we remind them that this person too has a mother.

In a similar way, if we wish to avoid dehumanizing Christ, we must remember that He too has a mother. We have a tendency to dehumanize heroes as well as villains. In action movies, our hero is frequently a character who was orphaned in childhood. It is as though we feel the need to take the parents out of the picture as soon as possible, because we cannot reconcile the helplessness, dependency, and innocence of infancy with heroism, strength, power, and might.

Similarly, some Christians like to ignore the fact that, having taken on the fullness of humanity, Christ too was a baby who cried, an infant who, like any other human being, had to "increase in wisdom and stature" (Luke 2:52). Therein lies the revelation of God's amazing humility. As St. Paul writes:

> [He] did not consider it robbery to be equal with God, but made Himself of no reputation, taking the form of a bondservant, *and* coming in the likeness of men. And being found in appearance as a man, He humbled Himself and became obedient to the point of death, even the death of the cross. (Phil. 2:6–8)

If God did not shun the humility of a defenseless child, how much less should we despise frailty, weakness, poverty, meekness? Yet we dream of power and glory, forgetting that our Lord was born of a poor maiden and laid in a manger. That God is Almighty is only one characteristic of God; that He is humble is another, equally important, characteristic. This humility is what made our salvation possible: He came down to earth that He might raise us up to heaven; He descended that we might ascend; He humbled

Himself that we might be exalted; and He died that we might live forever:

> Your nativity, O Mother of God, has brought joy to the whole world; for from you shone forth the Sun of righteousness, Christ our God, annulling the curse, and bestowing the blessing, abolishing death and granting us life everlasting. (*Apolytikion of the Feast*)

We can follow Christ because He followed us first; ʾHe came to rescue us by becoming one of us and has raised us up to the throne of His heavenly Father. The only reason we can call God "Father" is that the Son of God became our brother. This is why Christ was the only one who could give us the Lord's Prayer. Who else could bestow on us the "boldness to call upon You, the God of heaven, as Father, and to say: Our Father in heaven"?[2]

The Nativity of the Mother of God, like every

---

2   The Divine Liturgy of St. John Chrysostom

other feast of the Mother of God, points us to Christ, to the mystery of the Incarnation: God became completely human while remaining completely God, thus uniting heaven with earth and God with man.

> *Today has grace begun to bear fruit, revealing to the world the Mother of God, through whom the earthly and the heavenly beings unite for the salvation of our souls. (Vespers, fourth troparion of the stichera)*

We worship a God who, like all of us, had a mother. Because of this, we are able to call the God of heaven "Father." By being born of woman and through His selfless condescension, humility, and love, He has shown us what it means to be fully human.

✢ 2 ✢

Strength in Weakness

THE ELEVATION OF THE CROSS

On this day, we commemorate two events connected with the Precious Cross of Christ: the finding of the Cross on Golgotha and the returning of the Cross to Jerusalem from Persia. While in the Holy Land, the Empress Helen learned that the Holy Cross was buried underneath the temple of the pagan goddess Venus built on Golgotha. She demanded it be torn down and the Cross excavated. The search turned up three crosses. Uncertain which was the true Cross, the Patriarch Macarius ordered that each cross be placed on the corpse in a funeral procession passing by. The first two produced nothing, but the third brought the man back to life, thus determining that this was the very Cross on which our Savior brought life to the world.

Later, King Chozroes conquered Jerusalem, took the people into slavery and carried off the Lord's Cross to Persia. In 628, the Greek Emperor Heraclius defeated Chozroes and brought the Cross back to Jerusalem with great ceremony. Heraclius was carrying the Cross on his back when, suddenly, he froze. The Patriarch Zacharias saw an angel directing the emperor to take off his robes and walk with the same extreme humility with which our Savior bore His Cross. The emperor complied and was able to finish the procession to the Church of the Resurrection on Golgotha, where he restored the Holy Cross. (Synaxarion, Matins)

Ever since St. Constantine's victory under the banner of the Cross at the battle of the Milvian Bridge in AD 312, Christians have come to see the Cross as a symbol of power and authority. However, the Cross is not a symbol of earthly power, but of humility and self-denial; and Christianity is not a religion of conquest, but of mercy and meekness. Thus St. Paul writes:

> Therefore I take pleasure in infirmities, in reproaches, in needs, in persecutions, in distresses, for Christ's sake. For when I am weak, then I am strong. (2 Cor. 12:10)

Maybe we are tempted, as perhaps our Lord was, to respond to the mocking words, "let Him now come down from the cross, and we will believe Him" (Matt. 27:42). In other words, we may be tempted to think that true Christian witness and "success" is all about triumphing over the enemies of Christianity; and we Orthodox may think our mission in the world is for Orthodoxy to be established as the official church in every land. But spiritually, the Church is always strongest when it is persecuted; and whenever the choice is Christ or death, we witness not only false Christians falling away, but also average Christians being transformed into saints. The wheat is separated from the chaff in the face of hostility and oppression, and the Church is purged as in a fire.

To be a Christian is to deny oneself, take up one's cross daily, and follow Christ (see Luke 9:23), and this means that we choose meekness over might, forgiveness over vengeance, peace over anger, humility over pride, love over hate. We become true Christians when we crucify our passions, when we forsake our ego. To the world we may seem weak, but this "patience of the saints" (Rev. 14:12) is an incredible strength unmatched by the world, and which alone can change the world.

The fullness of humanity is given to us through the Cross, which is a denial of the self and the acceptance of death for the sake of everlasting life and union with our heavenly Father and Creator:

The Cross by its elevation called the whole creation to praise the pure Passion, the Passion of

> *Him who was elevated upon it; for having slain*
> *thereon him who had slain us, He brought to*
> *life us who had been slain, and adorned us and*
> *made us worthy to dwell in the heavens, because*
> *of the abundance of His goodness; for He is com-*
> *passionate. Wherefore, with gladness, we exalt*
> *His Name and magnify His infinite condescen-*
> *sion. (Vespers, first troparion of the stichera)*

Thus we Christians live with a sure hope and expectation and joy that no circumstances of life can take away from us. This is what St. Paul was describing when he wrote:

> But in all things we commend ourselves as min-
> isters of God: in much patience, in tribulations,
> in needs, in distresses, in stripes, in imprison-
> ments, in tumults, in labors, in sleeplessness, in
> fastings; by purity, by knowledge, by longsuf-
> fering, by kindness, by the Holy Spirit, by sin-
> cere love, by the word of truth, by the power of
> God, by the armor of righteousness on the right
> hand and on the left, by honor and dishonor, by
> evil report and good report; as deceivers, and

yet true; as unknown, and yet well known; as dying, and behold we live; as chastened, and yet not killed; as sorrowful, yet always rejoicing; as poor, yet making many rich; as having nothing, and yet possessing all things. (2 Cor. 6:4–10)

In weakness, we are strong; in tribulation, we are glad; in being hated by men for Christ's sake, we are loved by God. All that is accursed for the world is for us a blessing. Therein lies the joy and freedom of not being of this world; therein lies our strength and victory through Christ's sacrifice "for the life of the world" (John 6:51):

"In the world you will have tribulation; but be of good cheer, I have overcome the world." (John 16:33)

⤗ 3 ⤖

The Living Temple

THE ENTRY OF THE MOTHER OF GOD

Today the living temple of the holy glory, the glory of Christ our God, who alone is blessed and undefiled, is presented in the Mosaic Temple, to live in its holy precincts. Wherefore, Joachim and Anna rejoice now with her in spirit, and the ranks of virgins praise the Lord with songs honoring His Mother. (Second troparion of the stichera, Vespers)

On November 21/December 4, a week after the Nativity Fast begins, we celebrate the Virgin Mary's entry into the Temple in

Jerusalem, where, according to Tradition, she entered the Holy of Holies (the abode of the Ark of the Covenant) and where she dwelt in preparation for the Birth of Christ:

> Today the living temple, the temple of the great King, enters into the Temple, to prepare a divine abode. Wherefore rejoice, all you nations. (Festal troparion of Matins)

> Leading the procession into the Temple were virgins with lighted tapers in their hands, then the three-year-old Most-holy Virgin, led by her father and mother. The Virgin was clad in vesture of royal magnificence and adornments as was befitting the "King's daughter, the Bride of God" (Psalm 44:13–15). Following them were many kinsmen and friends, all with lighted tapers. Fifteen steps led up to the Temple. Joachim and Anna lifted the Virgin onto the first step, then she ran quickly to the top herself, where she was met by the High Priest Zachariah, who was to be the father of St. John the Forerunner. Taking her by the hand, he led her not only

into the Temple, but into the "Holy of Holies," the holiest of holy places, into which no one but the high priest ever entered, and only once each year, at that. Zachariah "was outside himself and possessed by God" when he led the Virgin into the holiest place in the Temple, beyond the second curtain—otherwise, his action could not be explained. The Most-holy Virgin remained in the Temple and dwelt there for nine full years. While her parents were alive, they visited her often. When God called her parents from this world, the Most-holy Virgin was left an orphan and did not wish to leave the Temple until death or to enter into marriage. The Most-holy Virgin Mary was the first of such consecrated virgins, of the thousands and thousands of virgin men and women who would follow her in the Church of Christ. Through the intercessions of the Mother of God, O Christ God, have mercy upon us. Amen. (Synaxarion, Matins)

The entry of the Mother of God into the Temple in Jerusalem marks the beginning of a radical change in religious history. The Holy of Holies, being the dwelling place of the Word of God, the Ark of the Covenant, was inaccessible to human beings, but now enters a woman to become the holiest thing on earth: the ark of the Word made flesh. Now the human body is the holiest thing on earth, and each of us is a temple of the Holy Spirit:

> "Believe Me, the hour is coming when you will neither on this mountain, nor in Jerusalem, worship the Father." (John 4:21)

> Do you not know that your body is the temple of the Holy Spirit *who is* in you, whom you have from God, and you are not your own? (1 Cor. 6:19)

As we ponder the wonder of God, who is infinite and who cannot be bound by the created universe, being conceived in the womb of a mortal woman, we are reminded of our exalted calling to be temples of the Holy Spirit, who cannot be contained:

Above the orders of the Cherubim, beyond the ranks of the Seraphim, you have been shown forth as more spacious than all of the Heavens, for in your womb you have contained our God, whom the universe cannot contain, and have borne Him in a manner beyond comprehension. Entreat Him, O Virgin, for us all. (Matins, Canon, Ninth Ode)

Let us believers exchange glad tidings, singing to the Lord with psalms and songs of praise, honoring His holy tabernacle, the living ark who contained the uncontainable Word; for in a supernatural manner is she offered to God as a baby. And Zachariah the great High Priest receives her rejoicing since she is God's abode. (Vespers, first troparion of the stichera)

The human being has become the temple of God. This is the calling of every one of us, male and female, young and old, rich and poor. In realizing this calling to be the dwelling place of the Holy Spirit, we discover the fullness of humanity: the image and likeness of God; we become priests of creation, charged with the special vocation of the first-formed to bridge and hold together flesh and spirit, sharing in both the animal and celestial kingdoms, binding together earth and heaven. This is what marks out the human being from the rest of the animal kingdom: Man alone has the power, the calling, the vocation, to act as priest and steward of the earth and to offer creation back to the Creator, for man alone is endowed with the image and likeness of God. Thus to be fully human is to be divine, and to give thanks and praise to the One who made us.

⇥ 4 ⇤

The Image of God

THE NATIVITY OF OUR LORD

*Come, let us rejoice in the Lord, proclaiming the
present mystery; for He has broken the middle
wall of partition, and the flaming spear shall
turn back, and the Cherubim shall admit all
to the Tree of Life.[3] As for me, I shall return
to enjoy the bliss of Paradise from which I was
driven away before by reason of iniquity; for
the likeness of the Father and the Person of His
eternity, which is unchangeable, has taken the
likeness of a servant, coming from a Mother
who has not known wedlock; free from alteration, since He remained as He was, true God,*

---

3   Genesis 3:24

*and became what He was not, having become
Man in His love of mankind. Wherefore, let us
lift our voices unto Him, crying, O God, who
were born of the Virgin, have mercy upon us.
(Vespers, first hymn of the stichera)*

We ARE SO ACCUSTOMED TO THE STORY
of the Nativity that it is easy to forget how strange
and amazing it is for God to be born. Christ is
eternally begotten of the Father, but as a Person
of the Trinity He cannot be born, since there was
never a time when He was not.

Yet there is more to the Nativity than the
paradox of God's birth. The Church also calls
us to wonder at the manner of His arrival upon
earth. Forget all you know of Christianity for a
moment, and consider: If God were to come
down to earth, what would it be like? How would
His coming be? Surely one would imagine, in the
words of *Ghostbusters*:

A disaster of biblical proportions . . . real wrath of God type stuff. . . . Fire and brimstone coming down from the skies! Rivers and seas boiling! Forty years of darkness! Earthquakes, volcanoes, the dead rising from the grave! Human sacrifice, dogs and cats living together, mass hysteria!

But no. Instead He chooses to be born as a little child, a defenseless baby. That same God of almighty power, whose presence, if manifested to us, really would be a disaster of biblical proportions, comes to us in complete meekness and humility. The One whose face "no man shall see . . . and live" (Ex. 33:20) becomes a baby for us, revealing to us all that is pure and good in humanity, and, at the same time, the humility of God.

We see in the Nativity the full meaning of humility, and in this humility, we see the true nature of God. For all that is truly good, pure, mighty, powerful, majestic, loving, and beautiful has no need to show off, no need to prove itself; it has no need to be compared to something else to be what it is. Thus God is not God simply because He is infinitely greater than we are, as though He needed us in order to be God; He is God because He is by His nature God. And so He comes to us in complete humility, in secret, poor and vulnerable. And in so doing He shows us that all that is truly good in humanity is also humble, and nothing more so than a newborn baby.

If we consider the true nature of God, we will find ourselves moving from the initial surprise that God came to us as a baby to the conclusion that there could be no other way. Only in a baby could the Image of God be revealed to the world, inducing not fear and terror, but love and tenderness, revealing to us both the humility of God and the goodness and purity of God's creation. To become fully human is to become like God, and to become like God is to "become as little children" (Matt. 18:3).

Purification & Enlightenment

THE THEOPHANY

When our Lord reached thirty years from His physical birth, He began His teaching and saving work. He Himself signified this "beginning of the beginning" by His baptism in the River Jordan. St. Cyril of Jerusalem says, "The beginning of the world: water; the beginning of the Good News: Jordan." At the time of the baptism of the Lord in water, the Father was revealed to the sense of hearing; the Spirit was revealed to the sense of sight, and in addition to these, the Son was revealed to the sense of touch. The

Father uttered His witness about the Son, the Son was baptized in the water, and the Holy Spirit in the form of a dove hovered above the water. John the Baptist witnessed and said about Christ, "Behold! The Lamb of God, who takes away the sin of the world!" When John immersed and baptized the Lord in the Jordan, the mission of Christ in the world and the path of our salvation were shown. That is to say: The Lord took upon Himself the sins of mankind and died under them (immersion) and became alive again (the coming out of the water); and we must die as the old sinful man and become alive again as cleansed, renewed, and regenerated. This is the Savior and this is the path of salvation. The Feast of the Theophany is also called the Feast of Illumination. For us, the event in the River Jordan illuminates, by manifesting to us God as Trinity, consubstantial and undivided. Also, every one of us through baptism in water is illumined by this, that we become adopted by the Father of Lights through the merits of the Son and the power of the Holy Spirit." (Matins, Synaxarion)

*F*ROM THE FEAST OF CHRIST COMING TO us as a newborn baby at Christmas, we move to the feast of Christ as a grown man revealing His divinity again in humility by taking the place of us sinners and receiving John's baptism of repentance:

> Then Jesus came from Galilee to John at the Jordan to be baptized by him. And John *tried* to prevent Him, saying, "I need to be baptized by You, and are You coming to me?"
>
> But Jesus answered and said to him, "Permit *it to be so* now, for thus it is fitting for us to fulfill all righteousness." Then he allowed Him.
>
> When He had been baptized, Jesus came up immediately from the water; and behold, the heavens were opened to Him, and He saw the Spirit of God descending like a dove and alighting upon Him.
>
> And suddenly a voice *came* from heaven, saying, "This is My beloved Son, in whom I am well pleased." (Matt. 3:13–17)

In biblical symbolism, water is a symbol of life and creation. And in descending into the waters of baptism, Christ cleanses and renews creation, and endows the waters of baptism with the power to purge us of our sins and renew us:

O Jordan River, why were you astonished to see the Invisible One naked? And he answers, saying: I saw Him and trembled; for how shall I not tremble and fear, when the angels trembled at the sight of Him, heaven was astounded, the earth was encompassed by trepidation, and the sea was bashful, together with all beings visible and invisible; for Christ has appeared in the Jordan to bless the waters. (Matins, second Kathisma)

Thus the first theme of the Theophany is purification and renewal, since our Lord will restore fallen man to the image and likeness of God by taking on a human body and deifying it by His own death and Resurrection, which is prefigured in His immersion in the waters of the Jordan.

The second theme of the Theophany is illumination. For in the Theophany the Triune God is revealed through the Person of the Son, the voice of the Father, and the descent of the Holy Spirit, thus enlightening us with the light of divine knowledge, with the revelation of the fullness of the Godhead:

> As You were baptized in the Jordan, O Lord, the worship of the Trinity was made manifest; for the voice of the Father bore witness to You, naming You the Beloved Son; and the Spirit, in the form of a dove, confirmed the sureness of the word. O Christ God, who appeared and enlightened the world, glory to You. (Apolytikion of the Feast)

> Today, You have appeared to the inhabited world, and Your light, O Lord, has been signed upon us, who with knowledge sing Your praise. You have come, You have appeared, the unapproachable Light. (Kontakion of the Feast)

Thus the Church calls us to renew our baptism

and to live up to our calling to be pure children of light. Just as no physical life is possible without water and light, so too spiritual life cannot be sustained if we are not perpetually cleansed and if we do not walk in the light of Christ. Without spiritual water and spiritual light, we cannot acquire full humanity; we cannot approach God, who is Himself Light and Life:

> Upon Galilee of the Gentiles, upon the land of Zebulon and the land of Nepthali, as the prophet said, a great light has shone, even Christ. To those that sat in darkness, a bright light has dawned as lightning from Bethlehem. The Lord born from Mary, the Sun of Righteousness, sheds His rays upon the whole inhabited world. Come then, unclothed children of Abraham, let us clothe ourselves in Him, that we may warm ourselves. You who are a protection and veil to the naked and a light to those in darkness, You have come, You are made manifest, O unapproachable Light. (Matins, Oikos)

⇥ 6 ⇤

What Am I Waiting For?

THE PRESENTATION OF THE LORD

Tell us, O Simeon, whom are you carrying in the temple in your arms with joy? To whom do you cry, shouting, "Now I have been allowed to depart; for I have beheld my Savior"? This is the One born of the Virgin. This is the Word, God of God, who was incarnate for our sakes, and saved mankind. Let us worship Him. (Vespers of the Feast, first hymn of the stichera)

MANY THINK OF THE THEOPHANY AS the conclusion of the season of Christmas. But the Synaxarion for February 2/15 makes it clear that the period of the Nativity really concludes with the Feast of the Meeting of the Lord, when we celebrate our Lord's entry into the temple forty days after His birth. Here the prophets Simeon and Anna, who have long awaited the Christ, finally meet their Messiah in the form of a child:

> Now when the days of her purification according to the law of Moses were completed, they brought Him to Jerusalem to present *Him* to the Lord (as it is written in the law of the Lord, "Every male who opens the womb shall be called holy to the LORD"), and to offer a sacrifice according to what is said in the law of the Lord, "A pair of turtledoves or two young pigeons." And behold, there was a man in Jerusalem whose name was Simeon, and this man *was* just and devout, waiting for the Consolation of Israel, and the Holy Spirit was upon him. And it had been revealed to him by the Holy Spirit that he would not see death before he had seen the Lord's Christ. So he came by the Spirit into the

temple. And when the parents brought in the Child Jesus, to do for Him according to the custom of the law, he took Him up in his arms and blessed God and said:

"Lord, now You are letting Your servant
    depart in peace,
According to Your word;
For my eyes have seen Your salvation
Which You have prepared before the face
    of all peoples,
A light to *bring* revelation to the Gentiles,
And the glory of Your people Israel."

And Joseph and His mother marveled at those things which were spoken of Him. Then Simeon blessed them, and said to Mary His mother, "Behold, this *Child* is destined for the fall and rising of many in Israel, and for a sign which will be spoken against (yes, a sword will pierce through your own soul also), that the thoughts of many hearts may be revealed." Now there was one, Anna, a prophetess, the daughter of Phanuel, of the tribe of Asher. She was of a great age, and had lived with a husband seven years from her virginity; and this woman *was* a widow of about eighty-four years, who did not depart from the temple, but served *God* with fastings and prayers night and day. And coming in that instant she gave thanks to the Lord, and spoke of Him to all those who looked for redemption in Jerusalem. (Luke 2:22–38)

Like Simeon and Anna, we all live with anticipation. We dream of the future; we look forward to meeting loved ones; we make plans for retirement; we hope for love, success, long life. Yet while we are bombarded with advertisements and advice about future planning, achieving success, acquiring wealth, and finding love, we are at the same time told to "live in the moment."

But is it possible to find real joy by living only for the moment? Is it not the case that, with the exception of sneezing, there is no real joy without anticipation of that joy? Consider the greatest sports matches you have ever experienced. You may have been rooting for your team or favorite player, never knowing which way the contest would go. You could not be sure of the result until the very final point was scored. It was frustrating and nerve-wracking, but also exciting and addictive. And your joy, when your team or player won, would not have been anywhere near as great if you had known the result from the start.

In other words, in every aspect of life, we must wait, endure, and look forward in hope if we are to experience real joy. The question is: What is the ultimate thing I am waiting for? What is it that is worth enduring so much anxiety and anticipation because the joy at the end is so intense? For Christians, the answer is: Christ and Resurrection. Thus we say every time we recite the Creed, "I await the Resurrection of the dead and the life of the age to come."

The prophets Simeon and Anna are a symbol of Christian life: anticipation, anxiety, frustration, doubt, longing, hope: then finally joy, fulfillment, complete happiness. But can we experience such satisfaction without all that longing and anticipation? Certainly not! We may all wish that life could be simpler and easier: everything we desire granted in an instant, no anxiety, no worry, no doubt, no tears, no pain. But the simple reality of life is "no pain, no gain." We must endure until the end to find true fulfillment.

This is what it means to experience the fullness of human existence, the beauty of love and longing. Life would be unbearably dull without anticipation. Christ offers us true life, which is the anticipation of joy, yearning for fulfillment. And when that yearning is finally satisfied, as our Lord promises us it will be, our joy will be beyond words:

> "Most assuredly, I say to you that you will weep and lament, but the world will rejoice; and you will be sorrowful, but your sorrow will be turned into joy. A woman, when she is in labor,

has sorrow because her hour has come; but as soon as she has given birth to the child, she no longer remembers the anguish, for joy that a human being has been born into the world. Therefore you now have sorrow; but I will see you again and your heart will rejoice, and your joy no one will take from you." (John 16:20–22)

❧ 7 ☙

The Servant of the Lord

THE ANNUNCIATION OF
THE MOTHER OF GOD

The Mother of God heard a language which she did not understand; for the archangel uttered to her the words of the Annunciation. And having accepted the greeting with faith, she conceived You, O God before eternity. Wherefore, we lift our voice to You in joy, saying: O God who was incarnate without alteration, grant the world safety and our souls Your great mercy. (Vespers of the Feast, second hymn of the aposticha)

THE SOLEMN SEASON OF LENT IS ALWAYS "interrupted" by a joyful and radiant feast: the

Annunciation.[4] This is when the Virgin Mary learned from the Archangel Gabriel that she would conceive by the Holy Spirit and bear the Son of God. Her response, after questioning the angel, "How can this be, since I do not know a man?" (Luke 1:34), was one of complete humility, faith, and acceptance: "Behold the maidservant of the Lord! Let it be to me according to your word" (Luke 1:38).

This response of the Virgin Mary should be the response of every Christian to the invitation to do God's will under any circumstances. "Behold the servant of the Lord" are words which should be inscribed on our hearts and minds: it is a statement not of arrogance or boastfulness; it is not a position we have taken upon ourselves, which makes us feel superior to "those other people" who, we think, are not servants of the Lord. Rather, it is a declaration of acceptance and

4　On the Julian Calendar, the Annunciation sometimes falls during Holy Week.

obedience to a request to belong to God and to do as He asks of us. This requires sacrificing our own will, our own self-governance. Accepting this invitation liberates us from the shackles of unruliness, ambition, and stubbornness, and enables us to accept whatever life throws at us with good grace: "Let it be . . ."

Because we want everything to be done our way, according to our hopes, our vision, our self-interest, we become bitter and frustrated when things do not go according to plan. The servant of the Lord, exemplified by the Virgin Mary, accepts what is not in accordance with his own plans. This acceptance is the key to true happiness, for certainly we are not in control of our own destiny. Like the rich fool of the Gospel (Luke 12:13–21), we plan and build in vain, thinking that everything is ours and that we are in control. The wise servant humbly acknowledges that true joy rests in the acceptance of a will greater, purer, and wiser than our own. He does not become attached to things of this world, knowing they are fleeting and can be taken from us at any moment; he does not assume that he will live to a ripe old age, knowing that death could be just around the corner; he does not seek to prevail over others, knowing that he is a humble servant of God who follows Him who died on the Cross.

When we make our own these words of the Virgin Mary, "Behold the servant of the Lord! Let it be to me according to Your word," we discover true freedom, true humility, and the fullness of human dignity.

❧ 8 ❧

Not of This World

PALM SUNDAY

The Word of God the Father, the Son who is co-eternal with Him, whose throne is Heaven and whose footstool is the earth, has today humbled Himself, coming to Bethany on a dumb colt. Wherefore, the Hebrew children praised Him, carrying in their hands branches, and crying: Blessed is He who comes, the King of Israel. (Vespers of the Feast, third hymn of the stichera)

"IF MY KINGDOM WERE OF THIS WORLD, My servants would fight" (John 18:36). So said our Lord to Pontius Pilate when he asked Him, "Are you a king?" Kingdoms are built with violence, oppression, and mammon. Christ's Kingdom is bestowed upon us through His self-sacrifice, humility, and poverty. His Kingdom is one that triumphs over death and evil. It is this triumph the people of Israel celebrated when our Lord entered Jerusalem after raising Lazarus from the dead when he had been four days in the grave. The Lord enters Jerusalem not on a chariot, with pride and pomp, rejoicing in the vanquishing of human enemies; He enters on a donkey, in humility, having vanquished death itself.

This double feast—the raising of Lazarus and our Lord's humble entry into Jerusalem a week before His own Resurrection—is what we celebrate at the threshold of Holy Week on Lazarus Saturday and Palm Sunday:

O Christ God, when You raised Lazarus from the dead, before Your Passion, You confirmed the universal resurrection. Wherefore, like the children, we carry the insignia of triumph and victory, and cry out to You, O Vanquisher of death: Hosanna in the highest. Blessed is He who comes in the Name of the Lord. (Apolytikion for Lazarus Saturday)

Give praise with one accord, O peoples and nations, for the King of the angels rides now upon a foal, and He comes to smite His enemies with the Cross in His almighty power. Therefore the children sing to Him with palms in their hands: Glory to You who have come as Conqueror! Glory to You, O Christ the Savior! Glory to You, our God, for You alone are blessed!" (Matins of the Feast, second kathisma)

The One who has power over death will hand Himself over to death that we may partake in His Resurrection—not merely a raising of the body from death, as was the case with Lazarus, but a new body that has been freed from our fallen condition and refashioned in the image and likeness of the God who took on the image and likeness of man:

> Let us come with branches to praise Christ the Master in faith like babies, purifying our souls and crying to Him with a loud voice: Blessed are You, O Savior, who came into the world and became a new, spiritual Adam from the first curse, and prepared all things for the best. O Word and lover of mankind, glory to You! (Matins of the Feast, first kathisma)

Mankind is committed to the pursuit of power, wealth, and conquest, but on Palm Sunday we are reminded that the weakness of God is greater than the strength of man (see 1 Cor. 1:25). All empires will fall, all conquests will fade, all wealth will dissolve, all flesh will return to the dust. And here comes one who having nothing, possesses all things (see 2 Cor. 6:10). He is our Lord and Master and Creator, and He comes on a donkey to proclaim the establishment of His everlasting Kingdom. Many expected the Messiah to be a vanquisher of the Romans, a mighty king of earthly power, charging Jerusalem on a steed with an army of tens of thousands. What a disappointment to see their hope of liberation arrive in such a ridiculous manner! But how profound that He should arrive in this way. What a powerful statement on the futility of human conquest.

Christ comes to vanquish death and to reverse the error of Adam. In this campaign for true liberation and conquest, the only blood that will be shed is His own, and so He enters Jerusalem not on a charger, but on a lowly animal bearing Him to His humiliating death. Christ comes to restore man to his full dignity by relinquishing His own divine dignity to human oppressors. Thus the celebration of Lazarus Saturday and Palm Sunday remains with us throughout Holy Week when we remember and relive our Lord's suffering and death—a celebration that will find fulfillment at Pascha, when we hear and proclaim the joyful news and announcement of true freedom and victory:

> *Christ has risen from the dead. By death He has trampled upon death, and to those in the tombs He has given life! (Apolytikion of Pascha)*

❧ 9 ❧

Children of God

THE ASCENSION OF OUR LORD

*When You came down from heaven to things on
earth, and as God raised up with You Adam's
nature which lay below in the prison of Hades,
You brought it to heaven by Your Ascension,
O Christ, and made it sit with You on Your
Father's throne, for You are merciful and love
mankind. (Matins of the Ascension, Kathisma)*

SOMEONE ONCE ASKED ME WHY THE
Feast of the Ascension is not a fast day. Per-
plexed, I inquired why he thought such a feast
should be a fast day. He replied, "Because the

Lord left humanity on this day, so surely it is a day of sorrow." This misses the point of the significance of the Ascension, which is not about Christ leaving the world, but rather about Him raising us up to the heavenly Father.

In ascending to God, our Lord took with Him our human nature, which He assumed for our salvation. Because He shares in our humanity, we share in His divinity; He is the first to ascend to God the Father in the flesh, thus paving the way for all of us:

> "I go to prepare a place for you. And if I go and prepare a place for you, I will come again and receive you to Myself; that where I am, *there* you may be also." (John 14:2–3)

If the purpose of the Incarnation is for Christ to restore us to the image and likeness of God, then this work is completed in the Ascension. As St. Paul writes:

He who descended is also the One who ascended
far above all the heavens, that He might fill all
things. (Eph. 4:9–10)

In the Ascension the divine destination of
humanity is made clear. Our Lord plans not only
to restore us to our former dignity and to the
earthly paradise that was lost, but to raise us up
to heaven: He grants us something even greater
than what we had before the Fall.

To be truly human is to be a child of God.
Therein lies the significance of the work Christ
came to do. Having become our brother, the Son
of God made us children of His Father:

"I am ascending to My Father and your Father,
and *to* My God and your God." (John 20:17)

Unlike other animals, human beings have a divine
vocation. We cannot be fully human if we do not
recognize and respond to that vocation. Since we
know that our true home and destination is the

throne of God, let our minds and hopes be fixed not on the earth, but on heaven above:

> *Abandoning on earth the things of the earth, leaving to the dust the things of the dust, let us now come to our senses and lift up our eyes and minds. O mortals, let our sight and all our senses fly to the gates of heaven. (Matins of the Ascension, Ikos)*

⤗ 10 ⤙

God with Us

PENTECOST

O Heavenly King, Comforter, Spirit of Truth, everywhere present and filling all things, Treasury of blessings and Giver of life, come and dwell in us, cleanse us from every stain, and save our souls, O Good One. (Vespers of Pentecost, third hymn of the aposticha)

*F*ROM THE ASCENT OF CHRIST FORTY days after Pascha, we are led ten days later to another divine descent—this time not of the Son of God, but of the third Person of the Trinity:

the Holy Spirit. He comes to dwell within us and to establish Christ's Church as a divine presence on earth, to shine "in our hearts to *give* the light of the knowledge of the glory of God in the face of Jesus Christ" (2 Cor. 4:6), and to make us "earthen vessels, that the excellence of the power may be of God and not of us" (2 Cor. 4:7).

If man's vocation is indeed to be divine, then our humanity is incomplete without the fullness of the Holy Spirit abiding within us. He makes us what we are called to be: temples of God, charged with being priests and stewards of Creation:

> *The Holy Spirit bestows all things: makes prophecies flow, perfects priests, taught the unlettered wisdom, revealed fishermen to be theologians, welds together the whole institution of the Church. O Comforter, of one essence and equal in majesty with the Father and the Son, glory to You. (Small Vespers of Pentecost, third hymn of the stichera)*

Through the Holy Spirit, we are able to experience the fullness of divine love, the union of God and man, of heaven and earth. Many think a perfect union with God is possible only after death, that the body is somehow a hindrance to this complete oneness with the divine. But Orthodox theology teaches that it is only in and through the body that man can achieve this theosis, this becoming God by grace.

We have already seen the significance of the human body in other feasts of the Lord: He was born of flesh, died and rose in the body, and ascended in the body for us. Now we see God choosing to live within our own bodies, divinizing us from within. The Son of God divinized human nature from within through the Incarnation.

Now this divinization continues within every baptized Orthodox Christian through the Holy Spirit. This is why our Lord said, "Unless one is born of water and the Spirit, he cannot enter the kingdom of God" (John 3:5).

To be fully human is not to escape the body, but to be with God in body and soul. This is why our Lord ascended in the flesh, to take the fullness of human nature to God. This is why the Holy Spirit makes us fleshly temples of God. And this is why, as we shall see in the following chapter, our Lord revealed to us the true potential of the human body in His Transfiguration.

11

The Human Body

THE TRANSFIGURATION OF THE LORD

Truly, He who spoke of old to Moses by symbols on Mount Sinai, saying, "I am who I am," has manifested Himself today on Mount Tabor to His disciples, showing in Himself the beauty of the first image, by taking unto Himself human substance. And He raised as witnesses for this grace Moses and Elijah, making them partakers in His joy and precursors of the Gospel of deliverance through the Cross and the Resurrection of salvation. (Vespers of the Feast, first hymn of the aposticha)

*I*N THE FIRST WEEK OF THE DORMITION Fast, we celebrate the radiant feast of our Lord's Transfiguration. According to the Gospel:

> Jesus took Peter, James, and John his brother, led them up on a high mountain by themselves; and He was transfigured before them. His face shone like the sun, and His clothes became as white as the light. And behold, Moses and Elijah appeared to them, talking with Him. Then Peter answered and said to Jesus, "Lord, it is good for us to be here; if You wish, let us make here three tabernacles: one for You, one for Moses, and one for Elijah." While he was still speaking, behold, a bright cloud overshadowed them; and suddenly a voice came out of the cloud, saying, "This is My beloved Son, in whom I am well pleased. Hear Him!" And when the disciples heard *it*, they fell on their faces and were greatly afraid. But Jesus came and touched them and said, "Arise, and do not be afraid." When they had lifted up their eyes, they saw no one but Jesus only. Now as they came down from the mountain, Jesus

commanded them, saying, "Tell the vision to no one until the Son of Man is risen from the dead." (Matt. 17:1–9)

Shortly before His Passion, our Lord reveals His divine nature. His divinity and humanity are inseparable. The light with which Christ is transfigured is a light with which His flesh is transfigured. Having become man, He is not revealed sometimes as man and sometimes as God, but always as the two at once. He is no less human in the Transfiguration and no less divine in the Crucifixion. Thus, according to the Synaxarion for the feast:

> So that His impending passion would not totally weaken His disciples, the All-wise Savior wanted to show them His divine glory before His passion on the Holy Cross. (This is why we sing the Katavasias of the Holy Cross on this day.) . . . Until then, our Lord manifested His divine power many times to the disciples but, on Mount Tabor, He manifested His divine nature.

> *This vision of His Divinity and the hearing of the heavenly witness about Him as the Son of God would serve the disciples in the days of the Lord's passion, in strengthening of an unwavering faith in Him and His final victory.*

Yet there is more to the Transfiguration than the revelation of His divine nature. Christ was transfigured not only to show us what He is, but also to show us what we will become:

> *When You were transfigured, O Savior, on a high mountain, in the presence of Your chief disciples, You shone forth in glory, symbolizing that they who are recognized for the sublimity of virtue shall also be made worthy of divine glory. (Vespers for the Feast, third hymn of the stichera)*

The Transfiguration of Christ points us to the glory of the Resurrection—a resurrection not only of the soul, but also of the body—and gives us a glimpse into that eternal and heavenly city which "had no need of the sun or of the moon to shine in it, for the glory of God illuminated it. The Lamb *is* its light" (Rev. 21:23):

> *Today on Mount Tabor You manifested, O Lord, the glory of Your divine image to the chosen of Your disciples, Peter, James, and John; for when they saw Your garments glistening as light, and Your face surpassing the sun in splendor, and they could no more bear to behold Your unbearable radiance, they fell to the ground, utterly unable to gaze upon it; and they heard a voice from on high testifying and saying: This is My beloved Son, who has come into the world to save mankind. (Vespers of the Feast, doxastikon)*

The human body is not an enemy or prison of the soul, but an agent. There can be no such thing as spiritual life without the body. Treating spirituality and the material world as two separate things flies in the face of everything Christ has done for us. Do we not eat His Flesh and drink His Blood at the Eucharist? When we think of spirituality, perhaps the last thing that comes to mind is the act of eating and drinking. But what can be more spiritual than this, when we eat and drink the Body and Blood of Christ? In other words, the Transfiguration teaches us that the body is sacred, and we must treat it as such.

It is for this reason that, on the Feast of the Transfiguration, we offer the first fruits to God that they may be blessed, and so that those who offer them and partake of them may attain joy and forgiveness. Just as these fruits grow and ripen under the rays of the summer sun, so may the spiritual fruits of faith and love increase and mature in us by the light of God's grace.

By that same grace, may we all reach some degree of transfiguration in life, albeit a small and invisible transfiguration of the heart.

12

Death Is No More

THE DORMITION OF THE MOTHER OF GOD

O marvelous wonder! The Fountain of life has been laid in a grave, and the tomb has become a ladder leading to heaven. Rejoice, O Gethsemane, the holy chamber of the Mother of God. And let us believers shout to her with Gabriel, the chief of the angels, saying, "Rejoice, O full of grace. The Lord is with you, granting the world, through you, great mercy." (Vespers of the Feast, first hymn of the stichera)

THE LAST GREAT FEAST OF THE CHURCH year is the Dormition of the Mother of God.

According to the Synaxarion for the feast:

The Archangel Gabriel appeared to Mary and revealed to her that within three days she would find repose. She returned to her home with great joy, desiring in her heart once more to see in this life all of the Apostles of Christ. The Lord fulfilled her wish and all of the Apostles, borne by angels in the clouds, gathered at the same time at the home of John on Zion. After seeing them, the Theotokos peacefully gave up her soul to God without any pain or physical illness. The Apostles took the coffin with her body, from which an aromatic fragrance emitted, and, in the company of many Christians, bore it to the Garden of Gethsemane to the tomb of her parents, Saints Joachim and Anna. Only the Apostle Thomas was absent, according to God's Providence, in order that a new and all-glorious mystery of the holy Mother of God would again be revealed. On the third day, Thomas arrived and desired to venerate the body of the holy and all-pure one. But when the Apostles opened the sepulcher, they found only the winding sheet, and the body was not in the tomb. That evening, the Mother of God appeared to the Apostles surrounded by a myriad of angels and said to them, "Rejoice, I will be with you always."

That the Mother of God was taken to heaven three days after her death is no surprise to Orthodox Christians. For "since you are the mother of Life, you passed over to life" (Apolytikion of the Feast). Yet while the Virgin Mary was an exception in passing so quickly from death to life, it is a destiny that awaits all the faithful. For this reason in the Orthodox Church we do not speak of "death" but of "sleep" (dormition is derived from the French word for sleep; the Greek terminology, *koimesis*, has the same meaning). When we go to sleep, we expect that we shall wake up; so too, when we die, we expect that we shall rise again.

Of course, Christians still die despite our Lord's Resurrection, but death is no longer the same: it is not "terminal." This is why we say that death has been destroyed by the Resurrection. Because Christ is Life itself, the very source of life, and therefore unable to be held by death, we are able to follow Him to the Resurrection and Ascension because we share in His humanity. He is the first-fruit of the risen and everlasting life to come, which His Mother was the first to share in, since it is through her that He entered the world.

St. Paul described death as "the last enemy *that* will be destroyed" (1 Cor. 15:26), and it must be destroyed because there can be no true life, no real fulfillment or everlasting joy, for as long as it remains. How can we be fully human if all we are will be dissolved and gone as though it had never existed? How can we be the image of the eternal God if we are nothing but dust and ashes? The fullness of our humanity cannot be restored until death has been abolished.

This is why we "await the resurrection of the dead and the life of the age to come" (Nicene

Creed). This is why we speak of death as sleep. For we live with a sure hope and expectation that body and soul will be restored, reunited, and renewed in Christ, and that "God Himself will be with [us] *and be* [our] God" (Rev. 21:3).

> And God will wipe away every tear from their eyes; there shall be no more death, nor sorrow, nor crying. There shall be no more pain, for the former things have passed away. (Rev. 21:4)

> Amen. Even so, come, Lord Jesus! (Rev. 22:20)

About the Author

ARCHIMANDRITE Vassilios Papavassiliou is a priest of the Greek Orthodox Archdiocese of Thyateira and Great Britain. He was born in London in 1977 and holds degrees in pastoral and social theology, classics, and Byzantine music. He is the author of the popular Meditations series (*Meditations for Lent, Advent, Holy Week,* and *Pascha*) and *Thirty Steps to Heaven* as well as the editor of the *Ancient Faith Prayer Book.*

Also by
Vassilios Papavassiliou

Meditations for Great Lent
Reflections on the Triodion
The Lenten Triodion exhorts us, "Let us observe a fast acceptable and pleasing to the Lord." Using hymns from the Triodion and the Scripture readings appointed for the season, *Meditations for Great Lent* shows us how to make our fast acceptable: to fast not only from food but from sin; to fast with love and humility, as a means to an end and not an end in itself. Keep this gem of a book with you to inspire you for the Fast and to dip into for encouragement as you pursue your Lenten journey.

Meditations for Holy Week
Dying and Rising with Christ
Archimandrite Vassilios brings his liturgical and devotional insights and warm, accessible style to

bear on the services of Holy Week, helping the reader enter fully into this most rich and intense period of the Christian year.

Meditations for Pascha
Reflections on the Pentecostarion

Far from being merely a "vacation from fasting," the Paschal season is a time that, properly understood, can greatly enrich our faith. During the Paschal season, we celebrate and rejoice in our Lord's Resurrection, and we prepare for the great feast of the Holy Spirit descending upon us.

Meditations for Advent
Preparing for Christ's Birth

The author of the popular *Meditations for Great Lent* takes us through the hymnography, scripture readings, and iconography for the forty days leading up to the Nativity of Christ, showing how a full understanding of the Incarnation can enrich our spiritual lives.

Thirty Steps to Heaven
The Ladder of Divine Ascent
for All Walks of Life
Many laypeople have attempted to read the great spiritual classic *The Ladder of Divine Ascent,* but have been frustrated in attempting to apply the lessons of this monastic text to their everyday lives in the world. In *Thirty Steps to Heaven,* Archimandrite Vassilios interprets the *Ladder* for the ordinary Christian without sacrificing any of its beauty and power. Now you too can accept the challenge offered by St. John Climacus to ascend closer to God with each passing day.

The Ancient Faith Prayer Book
Edited by Archimandrite Vassilios Papavassiliou, the *Ancient Faith Prayer Book* brings together the most ancient and popular prayers of Orthodox Christians with some additions that address issues of modern life, all rendered in elegant contemporary English and presented in a compact format for ease of use.

Ancient Faith Publishing hopes you have enjoyed and benefited from this book. The proceeds from the sales of our books only partially cover the costs of operating our nonprofit ministry—which includes both the work of **Ancient Faith Publishing** (formerly known as Conciliar Press) and the work of **Ancient Faith Radio.** Your financial support makes it possible to continue this ministry both in print and online. Donations are tax-deductible and can be made at www.ancientfaith.com.

To request a catalog of other publications,
please call us at (800) 967-7377 or (219) 728-2216
or log onto our website: **store.ancientfaith.com**

 **ANCIENT FAITH RADIO**

Bringing you Orthodox Christian music, readings,
prayers, teaching, and podcasts 24 hours a day since
2004 at **www.ancientfaith.com**